Easter Ross
and the
Black Isle

complied by
Christopher J. Uncles

By the same author:

Last Ferry to Skye
Lochaber and the Road to the Isles

The Band, 1st Bn. The Seaforth Highlanders (Ross-shire Buffs, The Duke of Albany's). In 1778, Kenneth MacKenzie (Earl of Seaforth) raised a Regiment of Foot consisting of men from the Clans MacKenzie and Macrae. The title, Duke of Albany's Own Highlanders, was granted by King George IV in 1823, his brother Frederick, Duke of York and Albany, being Commander-in-Chief of the army at that time.

© Christopher J. Uncles 1998
First published in the United Kingdom, 1998; reprinted 1999
by Stenlake Publishing, Ochiltree Sawmill, The Lade,
Ochiltree, Ayrshire, KA18 2NX
Telephone / Fax: 01290 423114

ISBN 1 84033 0325

ACKNOWLEDGEMENTS

A book such as this draws together information from a vast array of sources, both oral and written. Unnamed kind people we came across 'on location' provided directions or information regarding properties which had vanished, and the Highland Constabulary at Muir of Ord put me on the track of lost Cabaan (page 34). Others responded enthusiastically to written queries or gave permission for photographs to be reproduced, and my sincere thanks are due to them:

Sqn. Ldr. David J. Carey RAF (Ret'd); Cromarty Courthouse Museum; Dingwall Museum Trust and Ian Macleod; Mrs Jean Henderson; Colin D. MacKenzie; Alison Matheson (Senior Registrar, Dingwall); Richard Stenlake; Tain and District Museum; Mrs Sally Trotter; David Watt (The *Ross-shire Journal*).

Except where otherwise attributed, all the material is from my own collection. Many photographs have come from the camera of the late Mr F.W. Urquhart of Dingwall and I am especially indebted to the holder of copyright, Eric Sutherland, who generously permitted a free hand in the selection of his grandfather's work reproduced here. Finally, to my wife, Angela, who again suffered a good deal in the cause of research and who prepared the manuscript, contributing much by way of interest and encouragement.

Early seaplane: a Blackburn 'Iris' off Invergordon, 1926.

INTRODUCTION

My previous books, *Last Ferry to Skye* and *Lochaber and the Road to the Isles* provided a glimpse of life during the final years of Queen Victoria's record breaking reign and into the twentieth century, in two adjacent, but very different, regions of Scotland. This third collection of early photographs concerns another area with a very distinct character all of its own – Easter Ross and the Black Isle.

Interspersed between Inverness-shire and Sutherland, Ross and Cromarty (also known as Ross-shire and now part of the huge Highland Region), has constituent parts often referred to as Easter and Wester Ross. Of the former county titles, it was the only one with a double-barrelled name, and one of only three counties whose shores are washed by both the Atlantic Ocean and the North Sea. Extending from the Black Isle in the east, across the Minch to Lewis in the Outer Hebrides (plus some smaller islands), the land area totalled a little over 2 million acres, and at the turn of the century the county had a population of less than 77,000, of which some 2,000 resided in the county town of Dingwall. The physical characteristics of the county as a whole vary enormously from coast to coast, but such details fall outside the scope of this book. Suffice to say that a fertile, gentle countryside, with peninsulas formed by the firths of Beauly, Cromarty and Dornoch, are the principal characteristics of Easter Ross and the Black Isle. Somewhat confusingly, the latter is neither black nor an island, and while differing explanations abound as to the origin of the name, some have more credibility than others. The old name for the Black Isle was Ardmeanach ('the middle height').

However, it is generally agreed that Easter Ross is one of the finest farming areas in Britain. The rich arable land and large fields yield bumper crops of grain and potatoes; store cattle are brought here for fattening from the somewhat poorer pastures of the west; lambs for wintering. With its well maintained hedgerows and woodlands, neat farmhouses and large estates, the region has an air of prosperity which is, perhaps, more apparent here than anywhere north of the Great Glen. The ancient Royal Burghs of Dingwall, Tain and Cromarty, and the compact little towns and villages have individuality, and 100 years ago they had dusty streets and horse-drawn vehicles. Now, as then, they have remained close-knit communities. From the small coastal villages and Cromarty's Fishertown, men went down to the sea in boats to earn a precarious living at the fishing, although by the turn of the twentieth century the industry had been in severe decline for many years. The best years had been, perhaps, earlier in the nineteenth century when, for every fisherman at sea, there were several men and women ashore making sailcloth, hemp rope, baskets and creels, baiting the long fishing lines and repairing nets. When the fishing was good, the vennels hummed with activity.

Tourism, too, was important. Victorian and Edwardian holiday-makers favoured select Black Isle resorts such as Fortrose and Rosemarkie, and came in large numbers to take the waters at Strathpeffer Spa. They also came to fish the rivers, play golf on the links and stalk in the hills. It was the heyday of rail travel, and even small villages such as Fortrose and Strathpeffer had their own little railway lines which were well used before the Great War of 1914-18.

As a painter might say, this was a 'landscape with figures', and at the turn of the century because labour was plentiful, this landscape teemed with people. Heavy horses worked the land, and both agriculture and fishing generated a demand for a host of allied trades and crafts on which they depended, but which have largely disappeared today (e.g. blacksmiths, wheelwrights, creel and rope makers, the local miller). For many, the times recorded here were hard. The unremitting daily grind provided little return for a life of toil and none of the luxuries or 'necessities' we take for granted today. Hours were long and it was difficult to make ends meet. That said, it was undoubtedly true that the pace of life was slower and more peaceful; people were close to, and more in tune with, land and sea, the ever changing seasons, and the annual tasks which needed to be performed. It was a time when son followed father into business, and traditions were strongly maintained. There was an aura of permanence, stability and social order, and in the class-riven society of Victorian Britain, everyone knew their place. Nowhere was this more marked than in 'the Big House' where often vast wealth and the below-stairs culture came face to face. The number of staff required to run the house would be large – a bevy of butlers, housekeepers, cooks, domestics and gardeners who (apart from all the purely gardening tasks), would be required to produce a regular supply of fruit and vegetables for the kitchen, and flowers for the drawing-room. On an estate, there would be an added requirement for a factor and all manner of estate workers, including ghillies and gamekeepers, whose main responsibilities would be to ensure that there was plenty of sport for the gentry throughout the fishing and stalking seasons, and most importantly, for the annual ritual which commenced on the 'Glorious Twelfth'. Such seasonal lettings were, and still are, a fundamental necessity for the economic well-being, and very survival, of 'the Big House'.

At this time, Great Britain was the hub of a huge Empire. A glance at a globe of the world would show that one third of it was coloured red; it was an Empire on which the sun never set. It seemed that nothing could seriously disrupt the settled order of life. But it did, and when it came, everything that had seemed permanent suddenly evaporated. It was cataclysmic, and in retrospect the Great War of 1914-18 was a watershed. The assassination of an unknown Duke in a little known part of Europe resulted in a war which unleashed profound economic and social changes in its wake, leaving the world order in chaos; nothing would ever be the same again.

News of the outbreak of war came to Easter Ross in August as the harvest was being gathered in. It had been a golden summer, one which would be recalled in years to come, but for many it would prove to be their last enduring memory of home. Mobilisation followed swiftly, and as elsewhere, men from Ross-shire flocked to join the course of action on which Britain had embarked. Many were eager for 'a go at the Boche', and were convinced it would all be over in a matter of weeks. But talk of 'Berlin by Christmas' faded swiftly as the largest armies the world had ever seen (before or since) faced each other to become literally bogged down in the deep mud, the water-filled trenches and shell craters of Northern France and Flanders. Conditions were appalling. New and enhanced weaponry – including the first ever use of deadly gas in hostilities – would ensure a special place in military history for the Great War. The resulting casualties were horrific and on a scale never seen previously, with tens of thousands of men killed and maimed in a single day, often without a yard of territory gained.

A whole generation was killed in this terrible war, and its effects bore especially heavily on small communities such as those in Easter Ross and the Black Isle. Gaps appeared in all walks of life and commerce; familiar faces were absent. Families that had not directly suffered a loss knew one that had; some had lost *all* their sons. Family businesses were left with nobody to follow on and the large houses and estates too, were often succession-less. Conditions on many estates slipped into a slow, but irreversible decline; land suffered through being unworked, and sporting facilities by being unlet resulting in unemployment for those whose living depended on the land. For country estates throughout Britain the formula was uniformly devastating – reduced or no estate income meant lack of maintenance, and, in turn, sometimes over many years, ultimate dereliction and the subsequent loss of many fine properties. The malignant processes triggered by the Great War were compounded by the Depression and slump of the 1920s and 1930s. After that last glorious summer of 1914, it was a changed world.

Local research often yields surprises and interesting situations. For example, a brass plaque on the platform at Dingwall Station records that a tea stall there served 134,864 servicemen with cups of tea between 20 September 1915 and 12 April 1919! Elsewhere, after a detailed discussion about one house portrayed here, the proprietrix enquired whether I would mind witnessing her signature. It transpired to be the sale and transfer document conveying the estate to a purchaser south of the border.

Such then is the background to this book. Space limitation has necessarily resulted in difficult choices with regard to the selection of material, but from the Black Isle to the Kyle of Sutherland, I have endeavoured to make the choice as representative as possible. The photographs have been arranged in three broad sequences based on the county town of Dingwall.

Christopher J. Uncles

Ness Lodge Freemasons' picnic, Lealty, Ardross, 15 July 1925.

DINGWALL TO STRATH CONON

The low hills to the north and south of Dingwall provide perspectives of the principal physical characteristics of the locality – the waters of the Cromarty Firth (top) and the looming bulk of Ben Wyvis (above) which lies 9 miles north-west of the town. For all its 3429 feet, it strangely fails to make an adequate impression of its height, giving the appearance of a moorland ridge of almost uniform elevation. When the summit is crowned with snow (a not unusual occurrence), the eye is automatically drawn to the ridge which can be seen from a wide area around the Moray Firth.

Until a little over 1500 years ago, the area between these hills was a tidal inlet of the sea. Subsequent changes in the river basin where the Peffery drains into the Firth, created dry land on which eleventh century Norse invaders established a local Parliament. The settlement eventually grew to become Dingwall, which was raised to Royal Burgh status in 1226. Later still, this thriving market town became the county town and seat of local government of Ross and Cromarty, amalgamated by the Boundary Commission in 1891.

A bird's-eye view from the Sir Hector MacDonald National Memorial, 1907. From the bottom of the photograph, Hill Street gives way to Castle Street at the intersection with High Street where, on either side, the Royal and National Hotels can be seen. A number of fine buildings are readily identifiable. Further to the right, the building under construction near the post office and church is the Commercial Bank, now the Royal Bank of Scotland. In the upper part of the photograph, the railway line to Strathpeffer and Kyle of Lochalsh runs across fields beyond the Peffery, while both rail and road routes to Caithness curve around the head of the Firth towards Evanton.

Erected by public subscription, the imposing monument to Sir Hector MacDonald stands prominently on Mitchell Hill, the land having been gifted to Dingwall by a former councillor of that name. A miniature railway was used to bring building materials up to the site. In this photograph (probably of late 1906), the stone balustrade and turret have yet to be built.

Quite apart from the opening ceremony which took place on 23 May 1907, the photographer also captured a fine array of hats! In the extreme top right of the picture, the stone lettering on the tower reads: This tower was erected as a National Memorial to Major-General Sir Hector MacDonald KCB DSO ADC, AD 1907.

Major-General Sir H.A. MacDonald KCB DSO ADC LL D

Hector Archibald MacDonald (1853-1903) was born the son of a crofter in Rootfield on the Black Isle. He
served his apprenticeship as a draper in Dingwall but joined the Gordon Highlanders as a private in 1870. His
career would have been noteworthy for one fact alone in that he rose from the lowest rank in the British Army
to become a General. He served with distinction and heroism in several theatres of war on the African and
Indian Continents, earning the sobriquet 'Fighting Mac', but his name is more immediately associated with
one action in particular, that at Omdurman in 1898. Sir Herbert Kitchener had overall responsibility for the
reconquest of the Sudan, and the taking of Omdurman became a key to this end. It was a bloody, savage battle
in the extreme, featuring hand to hand fighting and one of the last cavalry charges by the British Army, made
by the 21st Lancers. Colonel MacDonald, leading a mixed Egyptian and Sudanese brigade of less than 3,000
men, found himself cut off by a Dervish force six times that number. Fortunately the latter failed to
synchronise their attack, and after a complicated engagement, MacDonald and his men beat off and put the
opposing forces to flight. A veteran war correspondent reported: 'MacDonald manoeuvred and fought his
men with a tact, coolness and hardihood I have never seen equalled . . . had the brilliant, the splendid deed of
arms wrought by MacDonald been done under the eyes of a sovereign, or in some other armies, – he had
surely been created a General on the spot'. The Dervishes were annihilated, the whole of the Nile Valley
passed into British hands and the murder of General Gordon at Khartoum in 1885 was avenged. MacDonald
was promoted to the rank of Major-General and knighted by King Edward VII on 13 May 1901. This was the
high-water-mark of a glittering career. Two years later grave charges were brought against him which resulted
in his suicide at the Hotel Regina in Paris on 25 March 1903 whilst *en route* to face court martial proceedings in
Ceylon. His remains were returned to Scotland in a sealed coffin which not even his next of kin was allowed
to open. MacDonald was buried in Edinburgh's Dean Cemetery but the customary military honours due a
soldier, let alone a national hero, were denied. Despite the funeral, there was widespread belief in the North
that their local hero was still living and, right up to the Great War, rumours abounded that Sir Hector had been
seen alive, or was working for a foreign power. The charges of which he stood accused, and vigorously
denied, were never substantiated.

Bugler Copping's funeral procession makes its way around the zigzag bends up to the cemetery on Mitchell Hill, 1908. This is one of a series of photographs depicting the Highland Light Infantry route march that year. In the distance, beyond the church, the regimental tents are pitched along the margins of the Firth.

The cannon on Mitchell Hill are fired to mark the Coronation of King George V, 1911. (Photograph reproduced here by kind permission of Dingwall Museum Trust.)

The Burgh Court House (known today as the Town House) pictured by Dingwall photographer, John Munro in 1890. The Tolbooth tower dates from 1730 and original plans for part of the ground floor included a schoolhouse, subsequently converted to the Town Gaol. Note the grilled and barred windows on the right and the shaft of the Mercat Cross on the left. The wings were reconstructed between 1903 and 1905 to provide Council Offices which link the Carnegie Hall and Library. They were further extended in 1926, being re-opened officially to commemorate the 700th anniversary of the gifting of Dingwall's Royal Charter by Alexander II. (Photograph reproduced here by kind permission of Ian Macleod.)

Town House, the remodelled frontage, 1911. Mr Frew's former chemist shop (left) is now the entrance to Dingwall Museum. Among the many interesting displays are a number of decorations, medals and swords belonging to Sir Hector MacDonald, and a Dervish cannon captured at Khartoum in 1898.

A number of photographs in this book have come from the cameras of two Dingwall photographers, J. Munro and F.W. Urquhart. Their studios were located in Harper's Court, a narrow lane off the High Street and their joint output over a period of some 60 years from the 1880s has made an outstanding contribution to the social history of the county.

John Munro (*c*.1851-1927) had a large family and his eldest son Hugh, born in 1876, was also a photographer. While the vast majority of his photographs were taken in the Dingwall and Strathpeffer areas, I have found examples as far afield as Kyleakin on Skye and Berriedale in Caithness.

Frederick Walter Urquhart (d.1947) served his photographic apprenticeship under John Munro and, after working in Glasgow, opened a studio of his own in Harper's Court in 1896. Apart from the usual photographic services, he offered photographic Christmas and New Year cards and portraiture by day or night, having introduced 'powerful artificial light' in his studio. His output was prodigious and I have seen examples of his work taken as far apart as Carrbridge, Culrain, Braemore and Kyleakin. Priced then at 1 ½d and later 2d, many of his postcards and

compositions are now highly regarded artistically. In addition to his Dingwall studio he also operated for a time from Tain and Strathpeffer. And he still found time to be a Bailie and Senior Magistrate! His studio camera can be seen in Dingwall Museum, but the old studios at Harper's Court were gutted by fire in the 1980s. (Photograph of F.W. Urquhart reproduced here by kind permission of Ian Macleod.)

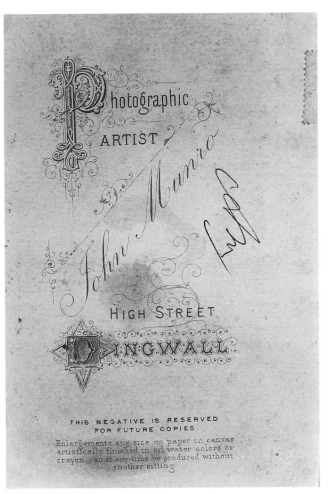

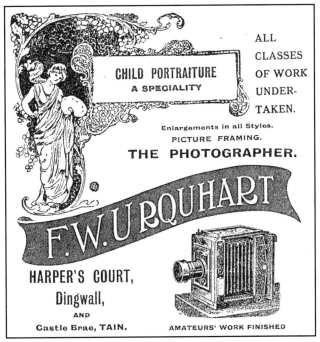

High Street, Dingwall. In 1906 a bottle of seven years old Ben Wyvis Pure Malt Whisky cost 3/ – and just 6d more for the ten years old. Tea cost anything between 1/- and 2/4d per pound.

Hill Street. The lettering on the roof of the Royal Hotel once read 'Gladstone Buildings'. The mother of the statesman William Ewart Gladstone, four times Prime Minister of Great Britain and Ireland, was born in Dingwall. When he received the Freedom of Dingwall he referred to the debt he owed to the town for this reason!

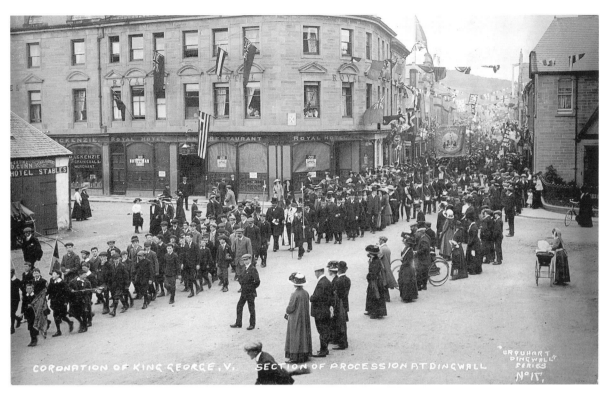

Part of the procession in the High Street, marking the Coronation of King George V, 1911.

Castle Street, 1906. On the right is the Episcopal Church of Saint James the Great. One of the Davidsons who owned Tulloch Castle had five wives, and they were buried side by side in a vault here. Sir Hector MacDonald's memorial on Mitchell Hill is under construction as indicated by the scaffolding still in place.

This mid-nineteenth century building, named Robertson's Hotel at the time of the photograph, was later renamed the National Hotel. (Photograph reproduced here by kind permission of Dingwall Museum Trust.)

National Hotel, High Street, *c.*1930. These former shops have since been incorporated as part of the hotel.

Post office and Commercial Bank, 1909. A previous photograph from the tower on Mitchell Hill showed the Commercial Bank (right) under construction; as might be expected, it is a classical and solid Edwardian building.

It is appropriate that the town should have a number of fine memorials to those who gave their lives in various campaigns over the last 100 years, especially as Ross-shire, and Dingwall in particular, was home to the Seaforth Highlanders. The Celtic cross at Ferry Road was erected by past and present officers and men of the Regiment in memory of their comrades who fell in the South African War of 1899-1902, mostly at Magersfontein Hill.

A detachment of 4th Seaforth Highlanders training at Kingussie in Inverness-shire, 1908. Six years later, such men would be fighting for their lives far from home in the most appalling conflict the world had ever seen.

Dingwall Station, August 1914. War has been declared and the 4th Battalion Seaforth Highlanders entrain for the front. For those departing, and for those who went to see them go, wish them luck and bid them farewell, this never to be forgotten day would remain etched on their respective memories. For many it would be their last goodbye. (Photograph reproduced here by kind permission of Ian Macleod.)

Station Road. This intricate, rustic cross made by the 4th Battalion Seaforth Highlanders in honour of their comrades who fell at Cambrai in November 1917, is a touching and unique memorial which once stood in the village of Fontaine-Notre Dame (France). It was, as H.V. Morton wrote, 'the only war memorial in Great Britain made by soldiers in the sharpness of their own grief, a rough cross set up in a foreign land for none to see but the peasants who would pass by, and perhaps tell their children how the Highlanders marched out to die at Cambrai.'

In 1924 it was decided to bring the cross home to Dingwall, where the unveiling ceremony took place the following year. Its inscription reads, 'No Burdens Yonder, All Sorrows Past; No Burdens Yonder, Home At Last'. (Photograph reproduced here by kind permission of Dingwall Museum Trust.)

Some time before the First World War, a little group pose for this photograph in Craig Road which at that time carried the main road to the North.

The Highland Light Infantry baggage train crossing the Dingwall to Skye railway line, 1908. Plenty of red tape to comply with, one suspects, before this operation was permitted by the Highland Railway!

Dingwall Town Band, photographed by John Munro *c*.1890.

Andrew Murray, Dingwall's award winning master baker. (Both photographs reproduced here by kind permission of Dingwall Museum Trust.)

'Snapshots'. A clever little title for this photograph of the Ross-shire Service Rifle Association, Dingwall, 1907.

The ladies wore white and scarlet. The Confection Stall at Dingwall Bowling Club's bazaar, 1907, must have been very eye-catching.

Many of the older generation often state that in the days of their youth, the seasons were more markedly different than those of today; summers were hotter and winters more severe. Whether there is evidence for this is difficult to say but 1906 was certainly noteworthy in Easter Ross. This photograph taken in October 1906 shows the first snow on Ben Wyvis; towards the end of the year what became known as The Great Snowstorm struck the whole area with dramatic results. Even earlier that year there had been heavy falls of snow recorded by Mr Urquhart's camera, no doubt with some difficulty.

Snowed up on the Heights of Docharty, February 1906.

Digging out on the Heights of Docharty,
February 1906.

Snow block at Auchterneed on the Skye railway line,
December 1906.

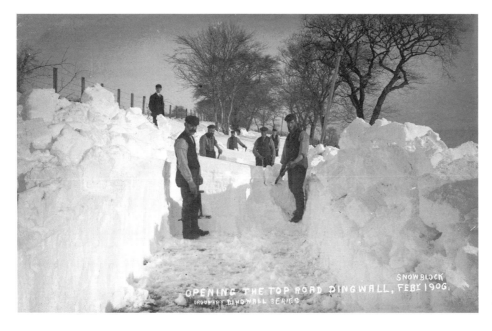

Opening the Top Road,
Dingwall, February 1906.

THE GREAT SNOWSTORM DEC: 1906.
CUTTING THROUGH A BLOCK ON THE SKYELINE,
HIGHLAND RAILWAY, AT AUCHTERNEED, NEAR DINGWALL.
COPYRIGHT "URQUHART DINGWALL" SERIES

GREAT SNOWSTORM DEC: 1906.
CLEARING THE BLOCK ON THE SKYELINE, HIGHLAND RAILWAY
NEAR AUCHTERNEED, "URQUHART DINGWALL" SERIES
DINGWALL.

The Great Snowstorm, 1906. The blizzard struck from the north-west about noon on
Wednesday 26 December. Its severity was such that drifting was instantaneous and road traffic
ceased within 30 minutes. The storm continued throughout the day bringing dense clouds of
powdery snow accompanied by a wind 'as keen as a whip-lash' and penetrating frost. The
Ross-shire Journal reported, 'Dingwall lay deep in snow all day and houses were white not only
as regards the roofs, but from top to bottom. Windows and doorways were drifted up . . . ' The
snowdrifts in the vicinity of Auchterneed Brae were fifteen feet high and the Kyle of Lochalsh
train buried here was finally extricated and brought back to Dingwall, from where it had
originally set out two days previously. No one could remember a storm of such intensity.

The qualities of the local waters had been recognised in the 1770s, but it was another century before the golden age of the Spa dawned. Those health-giving, curative and sulphurous springs, so beloved by Victorians, put Strathpeffer on the map. Medical journals of the day favourably compared the mineral waters here to those of Harrogate, Moffat and Aix-La-Chapelle. Various treatments were on offer, the waters advertised as 'strongly efficacious for rheumatism, scrofula, skin diseases and especially for affections of the liver and kidneys'.

Strathpeffer Station. Strathpeffer was becoming 'fashionable' and in the summer of 1885, a 2½ mile extension from Fodderty brought the railway line to a terminus in the village at this ornate station building. In later years travellers from London could connect at Aviemore with the Strathpeffer Spa Express, an immaculate train specially designated for the inland resort. The outbreak of the First World War hastened the decline of the Spa, and this train was withdrawn in 1915.

Craig Royston and Rosslyn Lodge, *c*.1905. Substantial Victorian villas such as these met the demands of those seeking restorative cures or healthy holidays in the cool mountain air. In 1910 the village had no spare accommodation; those Victorian or Edwardian visitors certainly knew how to holiday, coming for a month or more at a time. When they were not 'taking the waters' and the available treatments, they could play tennis or golf, fish the rivers, go for excursions or delightful walks, engage in a little sketching or painting, or just watch the world go by. And after dinner, if you had the stamina, there was invariably a concert . . .

The Highland Hotel, which dominates the village, opened in 1911. No less impressive internally, and typical of the age, are its cavernous public rooms. Foreign royalty visited, but by 1915 the Highland had closed its doors having been requisitioned as a military hospital. After the Great War visitors did not return to the Spa in their previous numbers; the halcyon days were over.

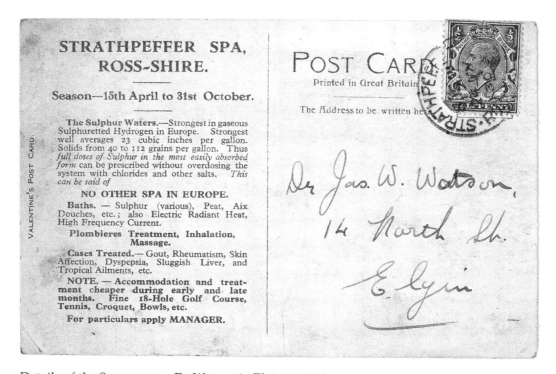

Details of the Spa sent to a Dr Watson in Elgin in 1930.

Pump Room, Strathpeffer Spa

'The Pump Room is prettily situated in the midst of the village; all the springs are under the same roof. There are about 20 Baths – mineral or plain water – hot, cold douche, showers etc. Charges: 1/- plain water; 2/- mineral. Reduction for a course.' (Extracts from M.J.B. Baddeley's *Thorough Guide*, 1884.)

The Square, 1909. Staff pose for this photograph outside the post office. Next door is the shop of George Souter (Stationer). The Souter family had publishing interests (including postcards) and also operated businesses in Dingwall. The photographs are linked by a facsimile post office cancellation stamp, presumably noting the time and date of the picture – an original touch.

First aeroplane flight in the Highlands. Mr B.C. Hucks at Strathpeffer Games Aug 24th 1912 with the Daily Mail "Firefly". No 15. Urquhart, Dingwall, Series

The aviator, B.C. Hucks, of the Royal Aero Club, made the first aeroplane flight in the Highlands at Strathpeffer in August 1912. Benny Hucks made a number of noteworthy flights that year with his 70hp Bleriot machine 'Firefly', sponsored by the *Daily Mail*. Its proprietor, Lord Northcliffe, had done more than anyone to encourage the development of aviation in Britain in its early days by sponsorship and the donation of large money prizes.

First Aeroplane flight in the Highlands. Mr B.C. Hucks at Strathpeffer Games Aug 24th 1912 with the Daily Mail "Firefly". No 10 "Gauging the wind" Urquhart Dingwall series

Long before the days of the familiar orange sock on airfields, gauging the wind prior to take-off was the personal responsibility of the pilot. Early advice to passengers included exhortations never to touch the propeller, to empty their bladders before leaving and to refrain from eating such foods as brown bread, peas or beans which were apt to cause formation of gas in the intestines.

The *Ross-shire Journal* reported; 'On the stroke of 3 o'clock the signal was given, the men let go the machine and the monoplane dashing forward at a great pace for about 70 yards, suddenly jumped into the air and with a wave of his hands Mr Hucks signalled that he was all right. The "Firefly" rose in the teeth of the wind and made towards Knockfarrel, which was covered with people desirous of getting a better view'. His flight lasted half an hour during which he ascended to 5,800 feet; he flew as far as Culbokie, returning over Dingwall. His perfect landing was regarded as a wonderful achievement by onlookers who greeted his safe return with acclamation. It was a day to remember.

'Tea etc, may be had morning and afternoon on Knockfarrel', (*Thorough Guide*, 1915.) And is there honey still for tea? No longer, alas.

Brahan Entrance Lodge.

Published by Souter, Stationer, Dingwall & Strathpeffer.
RELIABLE [WS] SERIES.

A fine pair of ornamental antlered stags surmount the sturdy pillars either side of the drive leading to Brahan Castle, *c*.1903. Once an early seventeenth century stronghold of the MacKenzies of Seaforth, the castle no longer exists. It was demolished in 1953, as foretold by the celebrated Brahan Seer.

BRAHAN CASTLE.

This postcard, written from Brahan Castle in November 1908, is marked 'the keepers and beaters at our last shooting party'.

Mr MacKenzie's General Store, incorporating Urray Post Office at the Marybank crossroads, is pictured here some time before the First World War. Advertisements for Fry's Cocoa and Sunlight Soap are visible, but of more interest, perhaps, is that at one time in addition to the store and post office, a tailor occupied an attic room and a coal merchant the cellar. The combined services must have made this building an essential lifeline to the scattered community in the Conon Valley. A beautifully glazed porch, saved from the demolished house at Rosehaugh (of which more later), has replaced the one shown on the left in this picture.

Built in the late sixteenth century on a ridge between the Conon and Orrin river valleys, the Tower of Fairburn was another MacKenzie stronghold. Now a ruin, it was last occupied about 1770.

Coul House, 1911. Sir William MacKenzie of Coul once owned lands of strategic significance around Contin. When the Dingwall and Skye Railway tried to negotiate a route to the west across his estates, he imposed unrealistically harsh and expensive conditions which resulted in the line being constructed through much more difficult terrain to the north. Strathpeffer became isolated and the railway company saddled with permanently high operating costs.

Falls of Rogie. Draining from Loch Garve, the River Blackwater plunges through a birch-clad rocky defile north of Contin. When in full spate, the rushing waters cascade downwards either side of a rock making an impressive picture.

Edwardian Fishing Party, *c.*1908. The one that didn't get away!

The River Meig joins the mighty Conon at Scatwell and for some 35 miles from source to sea, the river system winds its way along the fertile river valley of Strath Conon. Along its length are a number of noteworthy estates and productive farms, among them Scatwell, with its well maintained buildings – a model farm, photographed by John Munro in the 1920s.

An unusual item to bring this section to a close. The message on this postcard sent from Muir of Ord in 1916 reads: 'This is a shooting lodge belonging to this house; it's about nine miles away. We have to go to it on ponies as there is no road.' The huge Conon Hydro Electric Scheme implemented between 1946 and 1961 raised the waters of Loch Orrin. Remote Cabaan no longer exists; its ruins now lie *beneath* the reservoir.

THE BLACK ISLE

This section of the book takes us from Dingwall by the road south through Maryburgh and Conon, around the Black Isle to Muir of Ord. Before the First World War and in an age before the motor-car, nothing could have been more natural than this scene at the 'Spoutwell' on the Maryburgh road.

Residents of Maryburgh watch curiously as Mr Urquhart sets up his cumbersome camera equipment in the middle of the road to take this picture at least 90 years ago.

CONONBRIDGE. LOOKING TO BENWYVIS. (5)

Conon was a village once renowned for its flower-filled cottage gardens. On a warm summer's day, the scents were said to be exquisite. The River Conon, one of the finest northern rivers and famed for its salmon, flows out to the Cromarty Firth at Conon Bridge.

CONON BRIDGE.

Had matters turned out differently, Conon might have become an important junction serving a line running to the west through Contin planned in the 1860s and one to Cromarty in 1914. Neither materialised and the station closed in 1960.

Major-General Sir Hector Archibald MacDonald's birthplace at Rootfield on the Black Isle, c.1906.

The Black Isle is endowed with a number of fine properties; among them is this classical Georgian mansion, complete with Doric portico, at Newhall. Designed by Inverness architect James Smith, it was built for a Captain Donald MacKenzie in 1807 to replace an earlier house which had fallen into ruin a century earlier.

Poyntzfield House, built in the early eighteenth century and pictured here *c*.1906, was originally named Ardoch House. Successive additions between 1757 and 1790 produced a Georgian mansion, complete with courtyard. The name Poyntzfield followed the marriage of Sir George Gunn Munro to an English heiress, Miss Jemima Poyntz, daughter of Stephen Poyntz of Cowdray Park in Sussex. Poyntzfield lands were developed and improved with her family's fortune. Her name was given not only to the octagonal look-out tower whose cupola protrudes above the main roof, but also to the nearby village, Jemimaville.

The Rev. Donald Sage and most of his congregation left the Established Church at the time of the schism of 1843. He resided in Jemimaville and served the new Free Church for the remainder of his life. His book *Memorabilia Domestica* detailed the life and times of a Highland minister during these turbulent years. At the time of this photograph *c*.1907, the former manse was occupied by the local doctor.

In the 1820s, the small village developed laterally along the north side of the shore road overlooking the sandy, shallow waters of Udale Bay, an inlet of Cromarty Firth.

Udale House, at one time the village estate house, was severely damaged by fire. The site, subsequently levelled, is now largely overgrown.

Duffy, the chimney-sweep, on his rounds, *c.*1908. (Photograph reproduced here by kind permission of Richard Stenlake.)

'The Cromarty Railway so long spoken about has begun at last', is the message on this postcard mailed from the village in February 1914 after the first sod had been cut. The railway had been planned to run from the west side of the town, through Cullicudden to Conon, where it would join the main Highland network. But, despite the crowds, flags and bunting, all was not what it seemed. Just six months later, the outbreak of the Great War caused the scheme to be abandoned for good. The only visible reminders of this minor piece of local history are a few small concrete bridges spanning burns along the three mile length of the former track bed between Cromarty and Shoremill.

Two headlands, North and South Sutor, lie a mile apart either side of the entrance to Cromarty Firth's deep water anchorage. These sentinels guard the passage to the North Sea. During the First World War the Firth bristled with military installations, and anti-submarine net and boom defences stretched between the Sutors.

A fine view of the anchorage, packed with warships as far as the eye can see. Important overland routes also merged at Cromarty. An ancient trackway took a course from Beauly along the Black Isle ridge through Kilcoy and Killen to Cromarty, which was a stopping place on the Via Regia or 'King's Highway'. This medieval pilgrim route lay across the Firth (an ancient ferry crossing) through Nigg, northwards to St Duthac's shrine at Tain, and beyond to Dornoch and Caithness.

Above: Cromarty from the air, *c.*1930. Once an ancient Royal Burgh and former thriving seaport, the town we see today is largely the creation of George Ross who purchased the estate in the eighteenth century. Under his patronage Cromarty became 'the jewel in the crown of Scottish vernacular architecture.' Note the harbour, built in 1784 and, just below it, the large double storied four-sided complex (partially demolished in 1973) which housed the sailcloth and hemp rope-making works. One of Scotland's earliest factories in 1774, it gave employment to several hundred people in its heyday.

Centre: In the days of sail, Cromarty was a departure port for America. During the eighteenth century, large shipments of hemp and flax were imported from Russia to be spun and woven here. Exports included cloth, linen, rope, salted fish, nails and spades. One hundred years ago the fishing fleet numbered 66 vessels; today, there are none. The Royal Hotel, formerly 'The Admiral Napier', overlooks the quayside.

Left: For this sombre occasion flags are flown at half-mast; on the quayside, sailors with heads bowed await the cortège.

Built in 1783, the Gaelic Chapel is another public building attributable to George Ross. Pictured here, *c*.1908, it is now unroofed and deserted. The monument on the left was raised to commemorate one of the town's famous sons, Hugh Miller, born in 1802. Stonemason, geologist, Free Kirk journalist and author, his books are now collectors' items. He died in Edinburgh by his own hand in 1856, disturbed by the conflict between his scientific interests and his religious beliefs. His birthplace in Church Street is in the care of The National Trust for Scotland and open to visitors.

Built *c*.1772 on the site of the former Urquhart Castle, Cromarty House and its policies adjoin the Causeway, the earliest medieval route to the ferry point to Nigg. The Georgian mansion in the style of Adam is another legacy, courtesy of George Ross. An underground tunnel was built from the basement of the house to the Causeway so that servants and tradesmen could be neither seen, nor heard.

The vennels or narrow lanes of Cromarty's Fishertown were enclosed by Church Street (top) and Shore Street (above). In 1894, nearly 2,300 barrels of herring were cured here.

These fisher girls led austere lives. They baited the 500 odd hooks on the fishing lines with mussels, sometimes twice a day. Sea-boots were an unaffordable luxury for many, and the women were obliged to carry their menfolk on their backs out to the boats so that they could start the day with dry feet! At the day's end, they would bring the catch in baskets from boat to shore. And, of course, there were always mouths to feed; it was difficult to make ends meet. Little wonder that a coming generation sought alternative employment, a fact which hastened the decline of the Cromarty fishings.

Gordons Lane. A barefoot child, creels, barrels and boxes by doorways – everything you might expect to see in Fishertown. Note, on the right, drying fish for home use – perhaps small whiting or cod of no commercial value – hanging on a 'speet', either side of the doorway.

This is where my car is standing

H. HOME, Rosemarkie.

At one time Rosemarkie could boast several general merchants' stores, including this one in the High Street which also doubled as the post office. The eye is drawn to the classical frontage, but sadly this rather fine building had an air of permanent closure and was looking decidedly dilapidated on my last visit. Someone should breathe new life into it. Used as a garage at the time of this photograph *c*.1908, the building on the left is now a butcher's shop.

Street musicians in Bridge Street, *c*.1904.

FORTROSE LOOKING TO GOLF COURSE. M&S

Chanonry Point, the narrow neck of land protruding into the Moray Firth, is almost overlapped by a similar spit from the Inverness-shire side, just visible on the extreme left. The two lie a mile apart, and in medieval times this was a ferrying place, providing a link on the Via Regia (King's Highway), between Cromarty and Nairn.

Fortrose Pier. Inverness lay eight miles distant by sea. 'A good steamer has been put on to this route and those who enjoy a pleasant sail in calm water and amid softly beautiful scenery will not repent of devoting a few hours to the excursion. Passengers are allowed about three hours at Fortrose, during which they may visit the charming scenery of St Helena, or enjoy a capital bathe on the sands of Rosemarkie, one mile distant'. (Extracts: M.J.B. Baddeley's *Thorough Guide*, 1884.)

Edwardian elegance; St Katharine's, 1907.

Fortrose Station, 1910. The route of the Black Isle railway from Muir of Ord was a leisurely delight, threading its way through woods and farmland, enhanced in summer by the yellow of broom and golden ripening corn. There were stops at four little country stations and tantalising glimpses of the sea before the final destination was reached at Fortrose. The end of a journey maybe, but for holiday-makers the start of many a happy visit to Fortrose, Rosemarkie and district. The railway closed to passenger traffic in 1951, but goods trains worked the line until 1960, after which time the track was lifted.

Avoch and Ormond Hill, *c*.1905. Old family names Jack, MacLeman and Patience predominate here, so much so that at one time they constituted 90% of the population of this ancient fishing village. Some street names carry the forenames of the MacKenzie families of Avoch and Rosehaugh. It is easy to lose a sense of direction in the narrow vennels known as the Dock (centre) as the houses face a variety of directions. It is said that smugglers of old used this confusion to advantage in evading the Excisemen.

Rosehaugh House. For a long time in the ownership of the MacKenzies, the Rosehaugh estate was purchased in the 1860s by James Jack, who later took the name Fletcher. In 1893, using the family fortunes founded on tea, coffee and rubber interests, his son employed the architect William Flockhart to design and build a magnificent mansion-house in red sandstone, which took on aspects of a French château. If the exterior was extravagant, the interior was no less so, being fitted and furnished with every comfort in the opulent manner of the Victorian age. Twenty men tended the large gardens and the home farm became famous for prize cattle. The stables once held 100 horses and ponies, and the estate even had its own seven-furlong racecourse. Foundations for an enduring dynasty you might think, but you would be wrong. The house, completed in 1903, was demolished in 1959; the estate remains.

Charleston, North Kessock

The minor road from North Kessock along the shore of Beauly Firth brings us to Charleston (above), a former fishing village which takes its name from Charles MacKenzie, the Laird of nearby Kilcoy who died in 1813. At one time Charleston was renowned for the quality of its meal, ground at the 300 year old mill. In the 1950s this was thought to be the oldest working mill in Scotland, and before it closed the famous 'Black Isle Meal' was supplied throughout Britain.

Redcastle lies within the high wall along the north side of the shore road. This once magnificent and imposing red sandstone castle, dating largely from the seventeenth century, is thought to be on the site of a fortress built five centuries earlier. Up to the Second World War it was claimed to be Scotland's oldest inhabited castle. Today, the view from the strangely silent, overgrown drive is dominated by a stark, roofless, windowless structure, its turrets gone and its masonry crumbling – a scene of utter dereliction. The condition of this listed building, of considerable local importance, has long been a source of serious concern. Neglected Redcastle requires a public-spirited benefactor – and quickly, too.

"The Shop" Redcastle.

Urquhart.
Dingwall

Milton of Redcastle is the estate village of the now derelict 'Big House'. Formerly a thriving community with a market stance, a variety of services were available locally which made for (almost) complete self-sufficiency.

To our loss we are no longer 'a nation of shopkeepers'. Pictured *c.*1915, this shop, at the nearby hamlet of Killearnan, has long closed; only ghosts of the past linger in this quiet corner of the Beauly Firth.

WAR MEMORIAL. REDCASTLE

The granite memorial to the two dozen people of this parish who gave their lives in the Great War stands outside the Free Church of Scotland in Killearnan at Newton crossroads. It serves as a constant reminder of the incalculable human loss to this small Highland agricultural parish. Their regiments, too, represent a cross-section of some of Scotland's most famous – the Cameron, Gordon and Seaforth Highlanders, Highland Light Infantry, Scots Guards, The Royal Scots . . .

NORTH TO GLEN CALVIE

Tulloch Castle

Tulloch Castle overlooks Dingwall from a hill to the north of the town; the photograph on page 5 shows the general perspective well. Built in the sixteenth century and much altered over the years, it was originally the seat of the Bains. In the 1760s the property passed into the Davidson family by marriage. Henry Davidson had made his fortune as a London sugar merchant and did much to develop the estate which remained in the family's possession until the early years of the twentieth century.

MOUNTGERALD, DINGWALL.

The Old Evanton Road, parallel to the shore road north but set higher on the south-facing slopes of the hillside, affords panoramic views of the Cromarty Firth. Mountgerald, lying between road and shore, was built early in the nineteenth century and is little changed from this photograph, although the glass porch has been removed. A visitor wrote from here in August, 1931: 'It is lovely here, our bedroom has three windows and is the one that has someone looking out of one. We look over great trees to Cromarty Firth and the Black Isle. We have had three glorious sunny days after fog first thing. Little rabbits come out on the grass in front. Sea-gulls and sea-swallows fly about on the shore when we go down from here'.

The Foulis lands have been held by the Clan Munro since the twelfth century and there have been several houses on this site. The present property dates from 1754, replacing one put to the flames by the Jacobites eight years earlier. A protracted family feud and spectacular legal wrangle which went to

the House of Lords in the last century, left the estate much reduced in size and the house shorn of its contents. Family papers and manuscripts were gratuitously destroyed, and it is perhaps remarkable that the house survived at all. A huge programme of restoration has been completed in recent years under the present ownership of the 29th Clan Chief and his wife.

Another in the 'Great Snowstorm' series. This photograph shows the temporary stranding of a train heading north, between Dingwall and Foulis, in drifting snow on 28 December 1906.

Kiltearn Parish Church. From the sign 'Kiltearn Burying Ground', a narrow road crosses over the main A9 and winds down to the shore. Dingwall photographer, Mr Munro, stood with his back to the waters of Cromarty Firth to capture this idyllic scene, c.1905. On the left, the ornamental walled and gated burial enclosure (dating from 1588) containing memorials to the Munroes of Foulis is still there. But what of the church? Sadly, it is roofless and windowless, surviving only as a ruin. These days nothing but ivy, creeping higher year by year, encroaches on the external steps to the former Laird's Loft.

Three workmen in the narrow lanes of Milton of Katewell, south-west of Evanton, told us what they knew of the Glenskiach Distillery. Producing only small quantities of whisky, the plant had become uneconomic to operate and had closed during the slump of the 1920s. Voluntary liquidation followed and the distillery was demolished in 1933. Some stonework was reused in buildings and walls in the immediate locality, and the former distillery clock can still be seen mounted on a house nearby – a poignant reminder of a small industry which was once of importance in Glen Skiach.

Evanton village, originally named Novar after a local estate, was founded about 1810 and built a mile from the coast between two rivers which drain into Cromarty Firth. Structured on a grid system, the new village replaced the older settlement of Drummond. These two pre-First World War photographs of Balconie Street show the Post Office Stores and Novar Arms Inn (top) and the businesses of Geo. McDonald (Flesher and Grocer), the tobacconist and the cycle shop (above).

To the north-west of Evanton, the River Glass, plunging and rushing on its way to the Firth, has cut a narrow ravine through the rocks for some distance. The cliffs, covered with moss, fern and wood, rise to 110 feet and are so close in parts that the foliage almost meets across the river. An impressive sight after heavy rain when the flow is good and somewhat 'spooky' on a moonlit night, so they say!

Old maps of Easter Ross indicate a profusion of mills. In a landscape bisected by rushing burns to drive the mill-wheels, and fields heavy with grain, it is readily understandable that 100 years ago, the miller was someone of local significance. Many such mills have fallen into disuse and just disappeared, the only reminder of their existence being perpetuated in place-names such as Milton or Milntoun. This building at Culcairn has survived, but only as the Old Mill House.

(Top) Head of Loch Glass and (above) Wyvis Lodge and game larder (right), *c.*1906. Loch Glass is enclosed between steep hillsides and lies high up in the mountains behind Evanton, on the edge of Wyvis Deer Forest. Walter Shoolbred, a London cabinet-maker, built Wyvis Lodge in this remote spot in 1886. Unsurprisingly, the furniture and fittings, made in his own workshops, were of the highest quality; his firm eventually became the renowned Maple & Co. Ltd of London and Paris. Several loads of superb furniture, the like of which were rarely to be seen in Easter Ross, were transported north by the Highland Railway, hauled up Glen Glass by horse and cart and, on the last stage of the journey to the house, ferried the four mile length of the loch.

Eight miles east of Wyvis Lodge, as the crow flies, is Ardross Castle situated in less severe terrain. The millionaire Charles William Dyson Perrins (of Messrs Lea and Perrins Worcestershire Sauce fame), purchased the Ardross Estate in the 1880s. He immediately set about converting and enlarging the original house to create an ornate baronial mansion, filling it with his collection of art. The Great Hall, typical of the age, has a wealth of fine woodwork, oil paintings and stags'-heads. Mr & Mrs Perrins were benefactors to the nearby town of Alness where they were active in local community affairs. Both these photographs date to *c*.1907.

Is this structure a monument, a folly or just a monumental folly? Call it what you will, this exotic landmark on Fyrish Hill overlooking Novar House, was commissioned by General Sir Hector Munro (1726-1805), the owner of the estate, to relieve local unemployment in the eighteenth century and to commemorate

one of his famous victories. It is said to represent the Gate of Negapatam, a port in the Tanjore district of Madras in India, taken by the British in 1781. Later the estate belonged to Lord Novar, Governor-General of Australia, and the house was used as a hospital for wounded soldiers during the Great War.

Newton of Novar (Novar Camp), the small airfield one mile north-east of Evanton, 1926. Administered by Coastal Command, the Fleet Air Arm operated here in conjunction with the Invergordon naval base nearby. The aeroplanes on the ground appear to be Avro 504s. They were first used as fighters in 1914 (the observer being armed only with a revolver) and later had an important role as training machines.

The eighteenth century Old Parish Church of Alness, intact and complete with internal gallery, is shown here in the early years of this century. Today it presents a sad spectacle – open to the sky and derelict.

COMMERCIAL HOTEL, ALNESS.

(Top) High Street, Alness, looking west and (above) Commercial Hotel, Alness. Both *c*.1907.

A military funeral at Rosskeen Parish Church. Naval ratings pulling the gun carriage on which the coffin rests, pause in the lane outside the square, solid, early nineteenth century church between Alness and Invergordon.

There was a castle here in the thirteenth century and the small settlement was once known as Inverbreakie. Five hundred years later, the estate was purchased by Sir William Gordon of Embo whose plans led to the development of the harbour, advantageously situated on Cromarty Firth. He conferred a change of name to Invergordon which has survived to the present day. This picture of the long High Street shows the old post office and, just to the left of the drinking fountain, the town hall, photographed before the later development associated with the Royal Navy's substantial presence.

High Street, Invergordon.

'A big Naval Base is being formed here and the Government have acquired much land for fortifications. Special care must therefore now be taken not to trespass on their ground, else the consequences might be serious'. (*Thorough Guide*, 1915.) You have been warned! During the annual autumn exercises, for every Invergordon resident (about 1,000 in the 1920s), there were up to thirteen naval personnel aboard His Majesty's warships anchored offshore.

During the First World War, it was suspected that wide availability of liquor in specific military areas where personnel were working with ammunition and high explosives, might not provide a desirable combination. The Government of the day took control of licensed premises through the State Management District, or 'Carlisle Scheme', as it was also known, throughout the Cromarty Firth area, and incidentally, around Gretna. The Royal Hotel shown here, together with

ROYAL HOTEL, INVERGORDON

others at Alness, Evanton, Dingwall, Conon Bridge and Cromarty were drawn into this arrangement which persisted until about 1970. Control was exercised through the hours of opening; some critics went further, hinting darkly that the beer itself was not up to strength!

Mobilisation, 5 August 1914. Off to war with Germany. Brave men left to fight in a conflict they knew little about; many would not see their native land again. That fact alone gives this photograph added poignancy.

Late in December, 1915, the 13,500 ton armoured cruiser HMS *Natal* (built at a cost of £1.5 million) was anchored in Cromarty Firth, about a mile off Invergordon. The officers and ship's company were entertaining local civilians, including many children, at a Christmas party. Without warning, an enormous explosion, which could be heard 25 miles away, took the ship to her doom, together with 428 lives. The tragedy bore especially heavily on the population around the Firth, and the official enquiry reporting in 1919 after the lifting of censorship, suggested the cause to have been an internal ammunition explosion. Marked by buoys, the wreck was visible at low tide for many years afterwards.

Until about 1910, Invergordon had remained very much as envisaged by Sir William Gordon's plans. The harbour and port had grown in importance, and the immediate hinterland provided an orderly lay out of streets, overlooked from 1860 by the tall, slender church spire which dominated the skyline. In the years leading up to the Great War, Cromarty Firth's deep water anchorage came increasingly to the notice of the Admiralty, and massive development commenced on a major naval base. Coaling and oiling facilities (note the oil storage tanks) supplemented a floating dock and dockyard (foreground) capable of repairing the largest vessels. In 1918, U.S. Naval Base No. 17 was established at Dalmore nearby. During the 1939-45 war, the RAF operated flying-boat and marine craft units from there. It would be difficult to overstate the national importance of the whole area in two World Wars.

Warship HMS *King George V* in the floating dock, 1919.

H.M.S. "King George V" in the floating dock at Invergordon. Dec. 1919.

Three of the trades and specialist skills required by the naval base.

Coppersmiths, 1918.

Boilermakers, December 1918.

Engine Fitters Shop Ashore, 1916.

The memorial to the dead of one war overlooks warships keeping the peace, but maintaining vigilance and readiness for the next.

The War Memorial, Invergordon, showing Fleet.

Complex circumstances led to a brief mutiny in ships of the Atlantic Fleet at Invergordon in September 1931. The dire economic conditions, a legacy of the Great War, demanded savings and a 25% cut in seamen's pay was proposed. The threatened pay cuts would have borne disproportionately on lower deck men, cutting an ordinary seaman's pay from 2/9d per day to 2/- per day; in the end a 10% reduction was imposed. Poor communication and weak leadership resulted in men refusing to take their ships out of port for the annual autumn North Sea exercises. Solidarity was expressed between ships in the anchorage by cheering seamen massed on the forecastles.

At the time of the mutiny, HMS *Nelson* and her sister ship HMS *Rodney* were the largest and most powerful battleships in the world. *Nelson* was flagship of the Atlantic Fleet. Over 700 feet in length, with a complement of 1,314, she sat low in the water, her massive 16" guns radiating a sinister air. Eventually the men were persuaded to return with the fleet to their home ports, which was just as well, for the Board of Admiralty was actively considering plans to take military action to break the mutiny. The events at Invergordon shook the Establishment, and it is said that even today the very mention of the town's name in the corridors of power is enough to set alarm bells ringing.

HMS *Nelson*'s guns could project a one-ton shell twenty miles. The recoil was so shattering that they could not be fired in the forward position, only at an angle. A broadside rocked the ship in water; several of these in quick succession could result in instability and cause the firing ship to turn turtle.

Two undated photographs from Wood of Invergordon. The annual tasks on the land – drilling, sowing, hoeing (top) and harvesting were labour intensive, the work often involving the whole family. There was a strong spirit of co-operation in the countryside and neighbours often assisted, their help being returned similarly. Every estate or large farm had a team of horses (above) and they reigned supreme on the land until the Second World War when tractors began to replace them. Such everyday scenes are now but a distant memory.

Barbaraville, Delny, *c.*1900.

For generations there had been a mill at Milton (or Milntoun) near Tarbat, and in the eighteenth century the village was the centre of a thriving flax industry. Old houses and a former drovers' inn (left) surround a green on which the market cross has stood for 200 years. This photograph was taken *c.*1900.

Tarbat House, built for Major-General Lord MacLeod in 1787 is regarded as one of the most important Georgian country houses in the Highlands. Once an impressive mansion with finely proportioned rooms, its windows looked over Nigg Bay (an inlet of Cromarty Firth) to the Black Isle. This turn of the century photograph shows the house in happier times. In more recent years it has presented an unbelievably distressing sight, having been allowed to deteriorate into a roofless, windowless shell.

Kildary Smithy, *c.*1904. In a landscape dominated by the horse, it is hardly surprising that the village smithy was such a common sight and a vital part of country life. The continuous demand for shoeing, the repair of hand tools and other work, meant that the blacksmith's brazier was rarely out and the incessant noise of metal ringing on metal was a familiar sound drifting from the forge.

Balnagown Castle, Ross-shire

Historically, these were Ross lands and the earliest castle here is said to date from the fourteenth century. About 1820, the well-known architect, James Gillespie Graham, made substantial additions to the existing structure, this commission following the work he had undertaken for Lord Macdonald's new castle at Armadale on Skye. The 9th baronet of Balnagown, Sir Charles Henry Augustus Frederick Ross, died in 1942 aged 70 and at the time of his death, his estates extended to 356,000 acres. These had passed out of the family's hands by 1978.

In Victorian Britain extremes of wealth and poverty existed side by side. In stark contrast to the obvious wealth of the Laird of Balnagown, this old woman probably owned almost nothing apart from the clothes she is wearing. The bed in the corner and the few items in the stone alcove complete the austere picture, which captures so graphically the way in which many Highlanders lived at this time.

Enormous oil platforms, essential for the exploitation of North Sea resources, were constructed at Nigg in the 1970s, giving a spur to huge local development. In rather more tranquil times, this photograph, taken some 70 years earlier, shows the inn and to the left, Dunskaith House on the northern shore of Cromarty Firth.

Fearn Abbey. The present building dates from 1771, following a tragedy in which the roof collapsed 29 years earlier, killing 44 worshippers. However, the religious importance of this site extends over seven centuries when the area was settled by monks of the Premonstratensian Order; there are also remains of medieval chapels, one of which is shown in this photograph.

Balone Castle, near Portmahomack

Ballone Castle, situated on cliffs at the northern end of the Tarbat Peninsula, was once a magnificent structure enjoying an equally magnificent view over the Moray Firth. Built in the late sixteenth century as a fortress of the Dunbars of Tarbat, the castle has been in ruins for some 300 years. The cottages of the tiny village of Rockfield can be seen practically on the shore (extreme left).

Portmahomack

An Edinburgh lawyer, Sir George Mackenzie (1630-1714) once owned land hereabouts and he improved the little harbour at Portmahomack. Years later Andrew Carnegie (1835-1919), the millionaire philanthropist and owner of nearby Skibo Castle, a short sail away across Dornoch Firth, took a liking to the village and offered to buy it. In the event, his plan to turn it into his 'Venice of the North' came to nothing.

Morrich Mor is a large tract of sandy moor and desolate marshland, bordering Dornoch Firth, between Portmahomack and Tain. Up to the 1914-18 war, the area was used by the military for training, and periodic army camps were a regular feature. Indeed, at this time, various regiments parading through Tain, to and from the railway station or across the links, were a common sight. Later still, the RAF operated practice bombing exercises here, and the nearby village of Inver was completely evacuated in 1943 to provide suitable training for the 1944 Normandy landings. This picture shows civilians visiting the camp, *c*.1906.

Paradise Square, Tain, *c*.1907. These old cottages have been demolished; sadly 'paradise lost' now.

St Duthac's Chapel, 1891. The thirteenth century ruins of the chapel lie near the shore on the supposed site of the Saint's birth around 1000 AD. Duthac (or Duthus) died at Armagh in 1065, and following the subsequent 'translation' of his relics here, Tain (historically a place of sanctuary) became a shrine and place of royal pilgrimage on the King's Highway. King James IV is known to have made a number of such visits between 1493 and 1513. (Photograph reproduced here by kind permission of Tain and District Museum.)

Tain is considered to be the oldest of Scotland's Royal Burghs and in 1966 the town celebrated the 900th Anniversary of the granting of its Royal Charter. This substantial building in Tower Street was once part prison and houses the curfew bell. Built between 1706 and 1733 it replaced an earlier Tolbooth. Adjoining the tower, but out of view, Tain Museum and the St Duthus Collegiate Church are enclosed by Tower Street and Castle Brae.

Tain High Street. Looking towards the fine memorial to Kenneth Murray of Geanies (a Tain merchant, agriculturalist and banker) erected in 1879 (top); and from the monument to the Royal Hotel which forms the background to this photograph (above).

W Smith & Co., Tain

High Street shop fronts and mock timber framed
buildings, c.1904.

Tain Parish Church, formerly the United Free
Church, photographed c.1908. Its graceful Italianate
tower vies with the Tolbooth to dominate Tain's
skyline.

Princess Chrysanthemum, Tain
Royal Academy, 18 June 1909.

Lovat Scouts parading through the High Street, 1905. Formed during the Boer War by Simon Fraser (Lord Lovat) the Scouts had been recruited largely from the northern estates. They excelled with horse and gun and in country skills – tracking, stalking and the like. This postcard carries an intriguing note written by a Tain resident: 'Haven't much time, have had a terrible fortnight with the scouts and volunteers.'

2nd Battalion Seaforth Highlanders, on their route march, July 1911.

4th Battalion Gordon Highlanders marching up Castle Brae. This postcard was written from The Camp, Tain on 29 July, 1914, just six days before the declaration of war with Germany.

At the outbreak of the Great War in August 1914, the scenes of mobilisation we saw at Dingwall and later at Invergordon, were mirrored at Tain railway station. One can only wonder what was in the minds of these men as they went south by train, and across the English Channel to Northern France. One hundred and twenty-two of them never returned.

The Balnagown Arms at Ardgay is shown here after the substantial rebuilding and enlargement made in 1907. Under Mr and Mrs John MacLeod, the inn was generally acknowledged to be a splendid hostelry, and after her husband's death, Dolina MacLeod continued the business until her own passing in 1938. Much respected locally, immense numbers of people attended her funeral at nearby Kincardine. Do not look for the old inn today, for like much in this book it has vanished, in this case, having been destroyed by fire.

Ardgay railway station was at one time known as Bonar Bridge Station, even though the little town of that name lies one mile away over a bridge in the neighbouring county of Sutherland.

Timber loading bank, Ardgay Station, *c*.1917. As part of the war effort, some 400 American lumbermen came to the area to fell the coniferous forest between Creich and Bonar Bridge, where they erected great sawmills and bothies. These intensive operations also extended to Strath Carron, north west of Ardgay.

Beyond Strath Carron lies lonely Glen Calvie where our journey ends. The name of this glen has become a byword for one of the worst excesses of the notorious Highland Clearances. Glen Calvie was finally cleared in 1845 when eighteen families consisting of 92 individuals were ejected from their homes to make way for sheep. Their ancestors had occupied these lands for centuries; they were self-supporting and owed no rent. For days before dispersal, many

Carron River at Glencalvie, Ardgay.

had no alternative but to take refuge in the little churchyard at Croick where they recorded their plight by engraving their initials on a window pane – their memorial to a dispossessed people. The sadness here is deep, ingrained and almost tangible. Deserted for over 150 years, the silence of the empty glen is broken only by the sound of bleating sheep and the occasional plaintive cry of the curlew on the high tops.